Communicating with a Narcissist

Decode the Word Salad

SARAH SQUIRES

Copyright © 2019 Sarah Squires

All rights reserved.

ISBN: 9781081341985

DEDICATION

This book would be nothing more than an idea without the love and support of my friends and family who have always supported me.

My experience with a narcissist has been life changing. At the time all I felt was the painful loss of someone I loved deeply, but the situation became a catalyst to transformation. It has given me purpose and the space to work on my own wounds. I am a better person for it and am grateful for the experience.

Finally, I thank my Dad. For everything. I love you.

CONTENTS

	Acknowledgments	i
1	Introduction	1
2	Setting Boundaries	3
3	Self Audit	15

ACKNOWLEDGMENTS

Every single person who has trusted me with their story, this is for you. It is my hope that through sharing out stories, we help others through their journey.
I thank everyone who has gone before me and all those who come after me. Your strength to share your wisdom and growth is inspiring and so helpful.

1 INTRODUCTION

We all know trying to communicate with a narcissist is like trying to nail jelly - exhausting and pointless. They are expert liars and manipulators who love a good argument (even a fruitless one). They turn something which should be simple into a drama.

But before we delve into how to communicate with the narcissist, we need to understand their stance.

ATTENTION SEEKERS

It is the one element that separates narcissistic personality disorder from the other Cluster B personality disorders - their excessive need for admiration.

We often jump to the conclusion that this must mean they are Instagram addicts or power junkies but the truth is some crave YOUR attention above all else. They can be obsessive and jealous of everyone, including their own children. They constantly scream "look at me" and will behave terribly just to get your attention. You have heard the saying "even bad attention is better than no attention" and that is how a narcissist thinks.

As children they were given inconsistent affection and attention so their attachments are either disorganised meaning they both love and hate their need for others.

This can result in:

- Difficulty handling conflict with others
- Denies responsibility for wrong-doing
- Controls others through manipulative or overtly hostile ways
- Trouble showing empathy, remorse, trust or compassion with others
- Lack of the ability to give or receive genuine affection or love

All of which are easily identifiable as narcissistic traits.

So when they lash out and cause a drama, they are screaming out for you to take notice but perversely, taking notice simply gives them positive reinforcement that their poor behaviour gives them what they want - your attention.

This guide therefore will help you to not only reduce your own stress but also address their attention seeking behaviour.

2 SETTING BOUNDARIES

Everyone needs boundaries but narcissists more than most because they are essentially still children inside. Therefore when communicating with them it useful to think about how you would communicate with an infant rather than the adult they present as.

No/Low Contact

Limit your contact with them as much as is humanly possible. If you have children use a mediator or communication app. This reinforces that their behaviour is not acceptable and they will get no attention from you when they "misbehave".

Easier said than done right!? Especially when you have children. But here are some practical ways you can do this.

No Contact

No contact doesn't just mean not texting them or taking their calls. It means deleting their number, blocking them on social media and not asking your friends and family about them. You literally don't want any contact with them. This is by far the easiest way to move on because you have the space to heal. The quote *"you can't heal in the same environment you got sick"* is true. You need freedom from them and their mind games. If you give them the slightest morsal or contact, they will begin with the tactics of hoovering and love-bombing to get you embroiled once more in their drama. And you will set yourself back. Obviously if you have done this already or do find yourself back in it, that's OK. Relapse is somewhat inevitable as narcissistic abuse is like a heroin addiction. You want to feel the relief that they are offering. But remember it is short term relief. They are a drug and drugs are BAD!

My advice is to recruit a friend to act as your willpower. When you feel yourself tempted, reach out to your friend instead and they will bolster you to resist temptation.

Warning though, it will hurt. You will grieve. You won't understand why because your logical brain knows it is exactly the right thing to do but your emotional brain is craving the attachment. Allow yourself time to go through the stages of grief - anger, denial. bargaining, depression and finally acceptance. FYI the bargaining stage will be where you are most vulnerable to contacting them or snooping on their social media. Be aware of this and prepare yourself.

COMMUNICATING WITH A NARCISSIST

Also be aware that going no-contact triggers a deep trauma within the narcissist and so this will be the most active and dangerous time. They will try:

- Hoovering - narcissists hate to lose supply and so they will attempt to lure you back in. It will start innocently enough with some form of contact. Maybe a "can I collect my stuff?" or "my friend told me you weren't at work, just wanted to check you are ok". It's bait to see if you are serious about no contact. If you are, you will probably skip ahead to smear campaigns. If not, love-bombing comes next.

- Love-bombing - They will lavish you with loving messages, gifts, promises of how they realise the error of their ways and you are the only person they love. It will be like music to your ears after the pain of separation and it will absolutely trigger your own abandonment wounds. But it is the same lies they told you in the relationship, No-one can change in a few days or a week or even a month. Especially when it is a lifetime of behaviours. I know you want to believe them but the reality is NPD requires years of specialised therapy to address the disorder. If they really have been through that the likelihood is that they won't contact you because they understand now how much they hurt you and would never want to re-open that wound for you. So if they are back, they still lack empathy and simply do not care about the pain they caused.

- Smear campaign - you have resisted them so far and now they experience narcissistic injury. You have wronged them so badly that they have to punish you and they will use every means possible. Children. Friends. Family. Professionals. Pets. They will triangulate everyone into the drama and paint you as the abuser. In fact they will use your firm "no contact" rule as "evidence" of how abusive you are being - "they won't even talk to me to tell me what happened". This is designed to weaken your resolve and make contact as well as giving them a clear narrative that they aren't the problem, you are. Nothing you do or say to any of the flying monkeys will change the story. The absolute best thing you can do here is to remain "no contact" and ride it out. Give them nothing. A strong sense of self is needed here and if this is something you struggle with I highly recommend getting professional help from an experienced therapist.

When you step out of the abuser, victim and enabler triangle, the narcissist has no choice but to find someone else to fill the spot you left open. They may use your children so it is important to help build their resilience to withstand the pressure and use the techniques in the next section.

Low Contact

If you have children you will struggle to go no contact but there are ways for you to give yourself the space to heal whilst maintaining open communication about the children. Or the narcissist may be a family member who you aren't ready/willing to cut out of your life completely but recognise you need to limit your contact with them.

Set up a clear strategy for dealing with "emergencies" including what constitutes an emergency

You know the narcissist will do anything and everything to trample all over your boundaries and using the children is easy pickings for them. They will go against your requests but use the "it's about the children" or "it's an emergency" to lure you into breaching your own boundaries. This just provides them with the confirmation that they are powerful and in charge.

Emergencies could include:

- Health issues
- Unable to collect/return child(ren)
- Urgent appointment

Both of you need to agree to these but you if they are unwilling, have them as your own standard.

Also clearly state what and how the other party will be notified about the emergency. Again, narcissists love to keep control so they will often keep you in the dark about situations or communicate through a channel never used so that they can say "I tried to notify you, it's not my fault you didn't check". Make sure it is something you can access but isn't intrusive. So phone calls for example might be a definite "no" but a text is OK.

State what is to happen in the case of an emergency. Things to consider:

- Are they to be returned to the primary care-giver?
- Does the parent they are with deal with the emergency and notify the other parent on an hourly basis?

Remember to consider your own personal boundaries whilst ensuring that the children's needs are met.

Be clear on methods and times for communication

Be clear when and how communication can take place and enforce the consequences of not adhering to this.

If you have agreed calls with children with they are in the other parent's care, set clear times when the children will be available and on what platform. This can be agreed weekly, monthly or annually depending on the lifestyle of the parents. For example, someone who works shift work would need to have it agreed in line with when they get their rota. Do not accept calls or texts outside of these times.

Equally if you have calls agreed to the children when they are in their care, do not deviate from the times agreed. Even if they don't answer. A huge part of boundary setting is you maintaining them as well because the second you breach, the narcissist will see it as evidence that they can breach too. Yes it will be hard but think about the bigger picture and the long term peace you will get if you stick to it.

I recommend having one main platform for communication with the children with a back-up platform just in case. So Facetime is the preferred platform but if there is an issue with that, Skype. Nothing else unless agreed to by both parties.

Accept the losses

This is a tough one but the reality is, you will lose people through this process and may have to implement these strategies with people other than the narcissist. Particularly flying monkeys. The work I do with clients is always on building their own self-esteem and identity. You feel the pain of this so much more acutely when you lack a secure sense of self. This may be from your own childhood where you were perhaps not validated and so sought out that love and acceptance from others. Leading you right into the path of the narcissist. The narcissist knows this wound runs deep and uses it to hurt you and destroy you. Therefore it is so important that you heal your own trauma so that their methods have less power. I am not going to sugar coat this though. It does hurt. But you can recover and life a narcissist free life.

Grey Rock

Grey rock essentially means becoming as interesting as a grey rock. The narcissist needs information about you in order to be able to use it against you and remember they want your attention so the more they can actively involve you in conversation the better. Grey rock takes that away from them.

It is a level of communication which can be used as a gradual reduction of engagement with the narcissist. No contact is obviously very impactful and obvious. Low contact is like the final destination of where you have contact but you are in control of it. Grey rock provides the link road between the two. And subconsciously reinforces to the narcissist, gradually, that you are not worthwhile supply any more.

It involves you taking the emotion out of your communication with them and reducing your responses. They know your buttons so in every communication you attempt, they will be pressing them. Each time you react, it feeds their ego. When you begin to reduce those responses and limit your reaction you stop giving them what they need from you. Equally, it helps you to stop getting drawn into the drama. Making it easier to heal. It is really weaning you off the drug rather than going the cold turkey of no contact.

Simply put, less words. Be boring. Zero emotion.

It takes practice but it is highly effective.

Clear Instructions

Narcissists are adult children. They don't develop past their early years and this impacts their brain development. They struggle with thought processing, memory, emotional regulation, empathy. And they throw tantrums like a toddler. You know this, you have seen it. Well now it's time to use it to your advantage.

Think of them as children. In every situation, think how you would communicate something to a child. I am not asking you to nurture them like a parent would here by the way. Just to use this knowledge to adjust how you communicate.

In transactional analysis, we have three main states of being - parent (critical or nurturing), adult and child (free or dependent). In healthy adult relationships both parties communicate as adults as often as possible. However with a narcissist parties shift between the two parental states and the two child states. So when the relationship ends or you decide to go no/low contact you step out of those two states and into the adult state. But the narcissist remains fluctuating between the parent and child states depending on what they are trying to achieve. For example, a new partner comes along and they want to impress them and ensure that the new person knows that they are great and you are abusive so they adopt the critical parent state when communicating with you. Because you have done this dance long enough, you may well fall into the child state. This leads to conflict as you want to exert your independence and they want to control you. But to the outside looking in, you look like the problem. Because, let's face it, adults acting like children does look problematic.

Therefore it is important that you remain in adult state when communicating with them. The adult is rational and logical.

A great way to do this is by using simple, clear instructions. Follow these guidelines:

a. Be direct - "this has happened and this means…." Facts only and only the information needed for them to execute their task
b. Use clear and specific commands - "I need you to…" Give no room for negotiation
c. Give instructions one at a time - this gives them less room to take control
d. Keep explanations simple - grey rock
e. Give them time to process and repeat the steps if they have questions.

Use Closed Questions

Open questions are used to offer more response room for the other party. This is the exact opposite of what you want to do with a narcissist The less room you give them to respond the better. A close questions requires a simple "yes" or "no" response.

Rather than ask "would you be able to .... " try using "can you ...?" The different wording implies that you are questioning their ability and therefore a narcissist may be more inclined to prove their worth by saying "yes I can".

Give Options

Decide yourself on 2 or 3 options which would be acceptable to you and then offer them to the narcissist. This gives them the illusion of having some power. You don't need to give a thorough explanation as to why you have chosen that option. A simple "the first option is X which will result in Y".

It could be worth throwing in some reverse psychology here and implying the option you really want them to pick is the option that you definitely don't want them to pick. Narcissists love to cause you more work and do the opposite of what you want so by disguising what you really want under a "it's an option but I prefer not to" approach, you may find they deliberately choose the option you do want just to seemingly piss you off! Don't use this regularly though as they may cotton on.

Repeat

Do not get involved in a conversation. Simply repeat your options or instructions 3 or 4 times and then ignore them. This will teach them if they don't give you an appropriate response they won't get any attention. Children respond well to consequences and reinforcement. Therefore when you do get a suitable response, praise them for it. Stroke their ego. Not too much that they take it as a come on but enough that they get the boost. "Thank you so much for doing that" for example.

The bottom line is, communicating with narcissists does take effort. You need to be considered in your engagement both when you are initiating and responding. It may feel exhausting to start off with but if you stick with it, behavioural theory shows us that people's behaviours do adapt. Also remember that you are modeling this for your children and future relationships. These techniques are useful will lots of people, not just the narcissist. Change starts with you and so in the next chapter we are going to look at what you can do to reduce your own anxiety around communicating with the narcissist.

3 SELF AUDIT

Communication is a two way process so you also have to consider your own responses and perceptions. You have learnt in a relationship with a narcissist that your wishes and feelings are never heard and so with your new found strength you naturally want to have your voice heard. Remember that this is a reaction to the abuse and so take your time when communicating to assess whether it is your defense mechanisms kicking into place or whether there really needs to be a conversation. Also think about those parent, child, adult states we spoke about earlier. Take 5 minutes to reply to anything that is non-urgent (life threatening).

Every communication is going to create a reaction in you. It is therefore important that you are aware of some of your own triggers before you attempt any of the methods discussed. If you have a therapist, I recommend you go through these with them but the following sections provide you with some areas to focus on.

Rejection

The biggest difficulty with going no-contact is that you fear rejection. Bear with me on this one. Despite all the crap the narcissist has thrown at you and all the anger you have, your feelings were genuine and so it can be really scary to go no contact. You will miss them and you may even miss the drama yourself as you have been conditioned to accept it and perhaps even associate it with reward (narcissists push and pull and this can be addictive) but deep down you know that it isn't healthy for you to keep communicating with them. So if you find yourself reluctant to cut the cord, it would be worth examining your fear of rejection and move towards an acceptance that the relationship is over. There is no judgement in that. We empaths connect on a deep level so the attachment can be really hard to break and raise some of our own insecurities. That is OK, just recognise that and do what feels right for you.

Use your strengths

Getting to know yourself and your strengths (and weaknesses) is an important part of recovery. You've been told for so long how stupid, useless and crazy you are so this is a step in addressing that and those inner beliefs you may have developed. Spend some time really working out what you are good at and what you can do better. Be honest with yourself. Aim to work on the things you want to improve and do more of the things you're not so good at. For example, if you are great at holding your tongue during handover do more of that. If you struggle with texts, aim to get better at that.

Perspective

When you've been involved with a narcissist, everything gets distorted. The smallest thing is a huge drama, the big stuff is pushed aside. Take some time to really look at the big picture, see things for how they REALLY are. Rather than react in a knee jerk way, take 5 minutes and think about where it is coming from, what does it mean? IS IT IMPORTANT? Also realise that you are important. As is your time. Prioritise you and don't waste any energy on the drama.

Self audit

We tend to get annoyed by behaviour for a reason and sometimes it can be that it's a part of ourselves that we fear. For example, I hated the stalking and harassment because I know, deep down, that I have that weakness in me too. I have never done it because my strength kicks in but I have contemplated it because of my insecurities. So look at what it is about their behaviour and why it triggers you. It is actually really empowering to make that connection because you find your reaction changes. You are less impulsive and more conscious.

ABOUT THE AUTHOR

Sarah Squires specialises in empowering survivors of narcissistic abuse to life their very best life. She also trains professions to recognise Cluster B Personality Disorders, in particular the impact upon parenting.

She is the owner of The Nurturing Coach, NAPARRC Consultancy Ltd and COAP CIC.

If you wish you work with Sarah please check out the website at www.thenurturingcoach.co.uk

Printed in Great Britain
by Amazon